Piper Gets Her Period

SARAH HAUSLER

Copyright © 2020 Sarah Hausler

All rights reserved

Published in Australia by Bloom Wellbeing

Printed in Australia

First Edition

National Library of Australia Cataloguing-in-Publication entry available for this title at nla.gov.au

ISBN: 978-0-6487075-0-9

Cover and Interior Design: Swish Design

For all the 'Well Girls' everywhere

Piper Gets Her Period

SARAH HAUSLER

Contents

About this book   4

Section 1: Piper Gets Her Period   7

Section 2: Essential Information on Periods   33

    Quick questions and answers   34
    What's a period?   34
    Why do girls and women get periods?   34
    Do boys get periods?   34
    When will I get my first period?   35
    How often will I get a period?   35
    How long does a period last?   35
    Why is it called a period?   36
    Do all women get a period?   36
    Got more questions?   36
    Why do periods happen?   37

Section 3: Managing Your Period   41

    Using sanitary items   43
    Pads   43
    Panty liners   45
    Tampons   46
    Menstrual cups   47
    Period underwear   49
    Sanitary disposal bags   50
    An important note about disposing of sanitary items   51
    Making a period kit   52
    Keeping track of when you will get your period   54

Section 4: Other ways to take care of yourself while you have your period — 57

    What is self-care? — 58
    Symptoms of Pre-Menstrual Syndrome — 59
    Self-care ideas — 60

Section 5: A bunch of other questions about periods you might want answered — 63

    What's puberty? — 64
    Does a period mean I'm hurt or injured? — 64
    Will a period be painful? — 65
    My Mum got her period when she was 11 years old. Does this mean I will get mine when I'm 11 too? — 66
    Are there any signs that I might get my period soon? — 66
    Where can I buy or find sanitary products? — 66
    Who can I go to for help if my period arrives unexpectedly? — 67
    How long will I have my period for? — 68
    What are the reasons my period might stop? — 69
    When will I get my last period? — 69
    What if I don't want to get my period? — 70
    Is there any way to stop me from having a period? — 70
    Will periods be different for me because of my autism? — 70
    I'm feeling really scared about getting my first period? What should I do? — 71
    Am I allowed to talk about my period with other people? — 71
    What does 'flow' mean? — 72

Thank you, Acknowledgements & More info — 73

About this book

Are you nervous about getting your first period? Or maybe you've already started having your period, but you're finding it tricky to manage it by yourself?

Most girls worry about navigating their periods. Even though menstruation is a totally natural part of a female's life, it can still be daunting and challenging to manage.

Sometimes girls who have autism can find this time of life particularly challenging, as it is a big change in their body and life, and it requires the learning of new skills to take care of their body.

The goal of this book is to provide you with straightforward information about what a period is and why it happens, as well as practical advice on how to manage your period once it starts.

There are a few sections to this book:

- **Section 1** is an illustrated story about a girl called Piper, and her experience of getting her very first period
- **Section 2** provides essential information about periods – what menstruation is and why it happens
- **Section 3** provides information on managing periods, including using sanitary items and tracking your menstrual cycle

- **Section 4** includes information on looking after yourself when you have your period
- **Section 5** includes lots of answers to more questions you might have.

SECTION 1

Piper gets her period

This is Piper.

She's 11 years old. She loves soccer, graphic novels, her cats, and her two best friends, Taylor and Grace.

Piper has Autism, which means that sometimes she feels a bit worried and gets really, really upset when things in her life change or when unexpected things happen.

For the past couple of years Piper has been going through something called "puberty"—which is the time in every person's life when their body changes from the body of a child, to the body of an adult. In the past few years Piper has noticed that she started growing hair under her arms, and near her private parts, and that she also started developing breasts.

Piper has found going through puberty a bit tricky, and she's noticed that she's been a bit grumpier than she usually is. Her parents and her Occupational Therapist all told her this is a normal part of puberty.

This story is about another normal part of puberty—it's the story of the day Piper got her first "period".

What's a "period?" you might be wondering?

Well it's a special process that happens to women's bodies when they go through puberty.

Have a read of Piper's story, and then after the story you can keep reading the rest of this book, to find out all about:

- what a period is,
- why it happens,
- and how best to manage it when it happens to you.

*Remember, this is just the story of **Piper's** first period.*

*I can almost guarantee that when **YOU** get **YOUR** first period it will be totally different to how it happened to Piper.*

All people are different, and even though all girls will get their first period some day, it's rare that it will happen the exact same way for every girl.

It's a bright sunny day and Piper is playing soccer on the oval at lunchtime with her friends. Piper has played soccer for years, she's a striker— which means she kicks goals. She's an excellent player and she loves soccer and her teammates.

Piper, Taylor and Grace have been practising every lunchtime this week, because Sunday is the Grand Final, and they're determined their team will win.

But today, Piper feels a bit tired and achy, so she decides to take a break from playing.

No-one knows exactly when they will get their first period, it's always a surprise.

Read more on page 35.

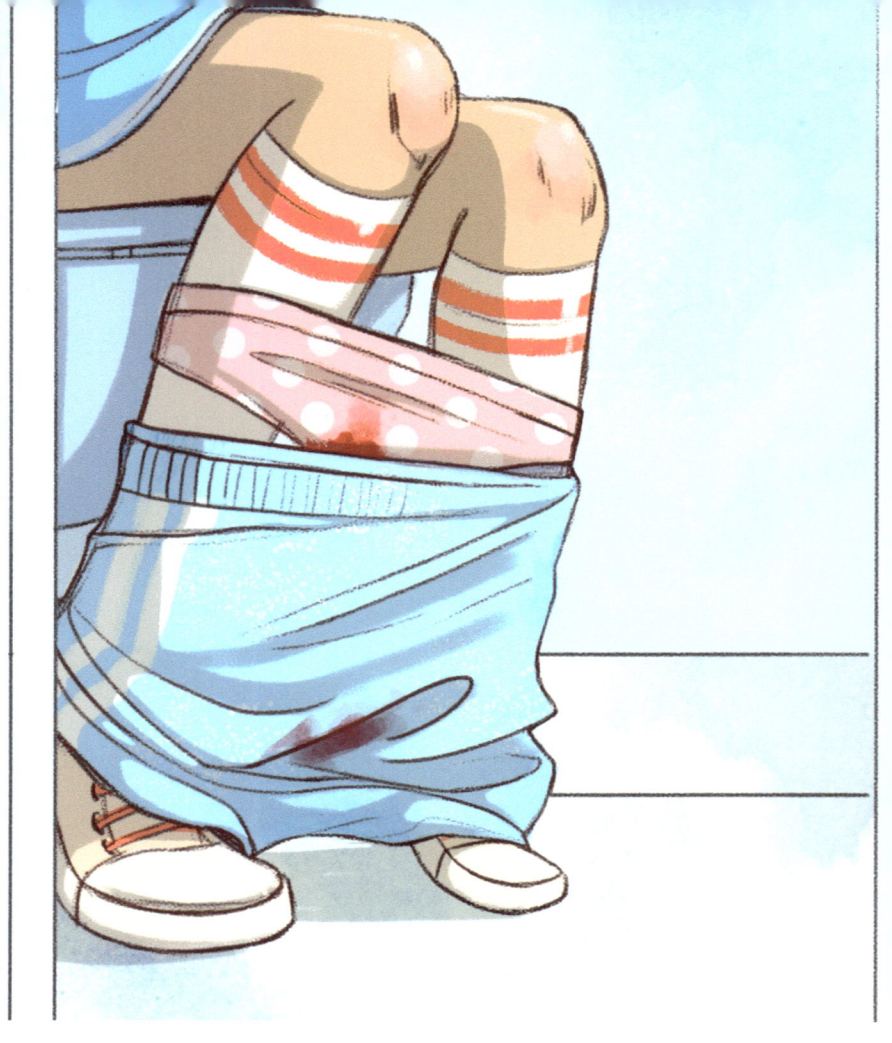

It's almost the end of lunchtime so Piper jogs to the bathroom to go to the toilet before it's time for class. When she gets to the bathroom and sits on the toilet, she notices a bit of blood on her knickers. There's blood on her shorts too.

At first Piper gets scared.

"I'm bleeding!" she thinks.

When she wipes herself, she notices blood on the toilet paper too. This makes her even more worried. But then Piper remembers a discussion she had with her mum recently.

"I think this might be my first period." Piper says to herself.

How much blood will there be?

Most girls get worried about how much they will bleed when they get their period.

Turn to page 40 for more information.

In the past year or two Piper noticed that her breasts had started to grow. She was also getting hair under her arms and between her legs, near her vulva.

Her mum had explained to her that this was part of a process called "puberty". This was the time in a girl's life when her body changes from that of a child, to the body of a woman.

Mum explained that puberty led to "menstruation", something that was also known as "getting your period". Mum had even pointed out the aisle of "sanitary items" at the supermarket.

Want to know more about puberty? Turn to page 64 to find out.

Piper and her mum had bought some special things that day. They'd bought a box of what her mum called "pads", some wet wipes and some hygienic disposal bags. They'd also bought a toiletries bag to store all the items in, along with some spare underwear. Piper's Mum called it her "period kit", and showed her that the pads were to be worn inside her knickers, for collecting the blood when she got her period.

"Of course!" thought Piper, "I've got the period kit in my school bag".

But Piper's excitement faded again when she realised her school bag was in her locker outside of her classroom. She didn't want to walk around the school with blood on her shorts. She didn't want the other kids to see because she was worried they might laugh at her.

What's inside all those packs and boxes in the sanitary aisle?

Turn to pages 43-51 to find out.

Piper felt anxious and alone. She didn't know what to do. What else had her mum told her that day? Piper closed her eyes and thought really hard, trying to remember. "If you get your period at school, you can go to the front office and ask the office ladies for help. They will have spare pads, and maybe a change of clothes for you." By this time, the end of lunch bell had rung and Piper figured all the other kids would be in class, so she quickly walked to the office.

"How can I help you Piper?" asked Alice, the office lady.

Piper looked down at her feet. She was so nervous, her hands felt clammy. "I think I just got my period, can you please help?"

And that's exactly what Alice the office lady did. She took Piper to the sick room so she could rest and gave her a pad and some spare underwear and shorts to change into. "Would you like me to call your parents to come and collect you early?" asked Alice, as she could see Piper seemed upset.

What if you get your period somewhere other than home or school? Who else can you go to for help?

Turn to page 67 for answers.

On the way home from school, Piper asked her mum, "Do I have to stay home from school every time I get my period."

"Oh no, honey," her mum replied. "I'm just picking you up early today because this is your first period. From now on we'll keep track of your period and you can make sure that you're prepared with pads when it's due to arrive."

Piper had so many questions in her head. She didn't know which one to ask first.

How do I know when to change my pad?

What does "track your period" mean?

Is this bleeding going to hurt?

Finally she asked her mum, "How long will I bleed for?"

"Oh, about five days," said her mum. "Since today is Thursday, that means you'll probably have your period until about Monday."

"Oh no!!"

Suddenly Piper got really worried and felt like she might cry. "But I've got soccer on Sunday. It's the grand final. I can't miss it!!" she said.

"It's okay Piper, you can still play," said her Mum. "Just because you have your period doesn't mean that you can't play sport or do other things that you love. You just need to pay attention to how your body feels. If you feel like you need a rest the coach can sub you out to have a break on the bench."

This made Piper feel a bit better, but she was still worried about how she was going to manage having her period for the next five days.

How can you keep track of your period?

Check out page 54 for more information.

That night, Piper didn't feel too good.

She was tired and had a crampy feeling in her belly. For some reason she felt really grumpy too.

Her older sister, Katie, suggested the whole family have a movie night. She told Piper to get her comfiest pyjamas on and lie on the couch with a heat pack on her tummy.

Piper's sister also made her popcorn and hot chocolate to have during the movie.

Piper wasn't sure why her sister was being extra-nice to her tonight, but it sure did make her feel better.

What are some other ways you can look after yourself when you have your period?

Turn to page 57 for more ideas.

The next morning, Piper was nervous about going to school. Was she going to be able to manage her period on her own? She'd done it a few times at home, with help from her Mum.

Piper didn't really like learning new things. It was tricky and made her brain feel like it was squeezed too tight. As her dad pulled up outside school, Piper double checked her backpack to make sure her period kit was there and filled with supplies.

"Do I have to tell my friends that I have my period Dad? Will they be able to tell by looking at me?" she asked.

"Oh no honey, they won't know unless you tell them, and it's totally up to you if you tell them. It's your body, so it's your choice," said her Dad.

"Thanks Dad." said Piper as she got out of the car.

"Love you kiddo!" yelled her Dad back.

"Ugh, Dad, you're so embarrassing!" said Piper, as she laughed and ran off to meet her friends.

What might you want to pack in your "period kit"? Turn to page 53 for some ideas.

Piper woke up on Sunday morning and noticed that while she still had her period, there seemed to be less blood than there had been the first few days. She was happy about this as she remembered it meant that her period would be finishing soon. The crampy feelings in Piper's belly had also gone away in the last day or two. But now that feeling was replaced with another one—butterflies!! Piper felt like a million butterflies were swooping around inside her stomach. It always felt like this when she was nervous, and today she was super-nervous, because it was the day of her soccer grand final.

Piper pulled her soccer kit on, and tapped her fingers on her knee for the whole drive to the ground. When the whistle blew to start the game Piper forgot all about having her period, because she was 100 percent focused on playing her best for her team.

The match was close, but when the referee finally blew her whistle to end the match, Piper's team had won the game, three goals to two! Piper was so, so excited, and she felt happier than she ever had in her entire life. Having her period wasn't going to stop her doing anything, not even winning the soccer grand final!

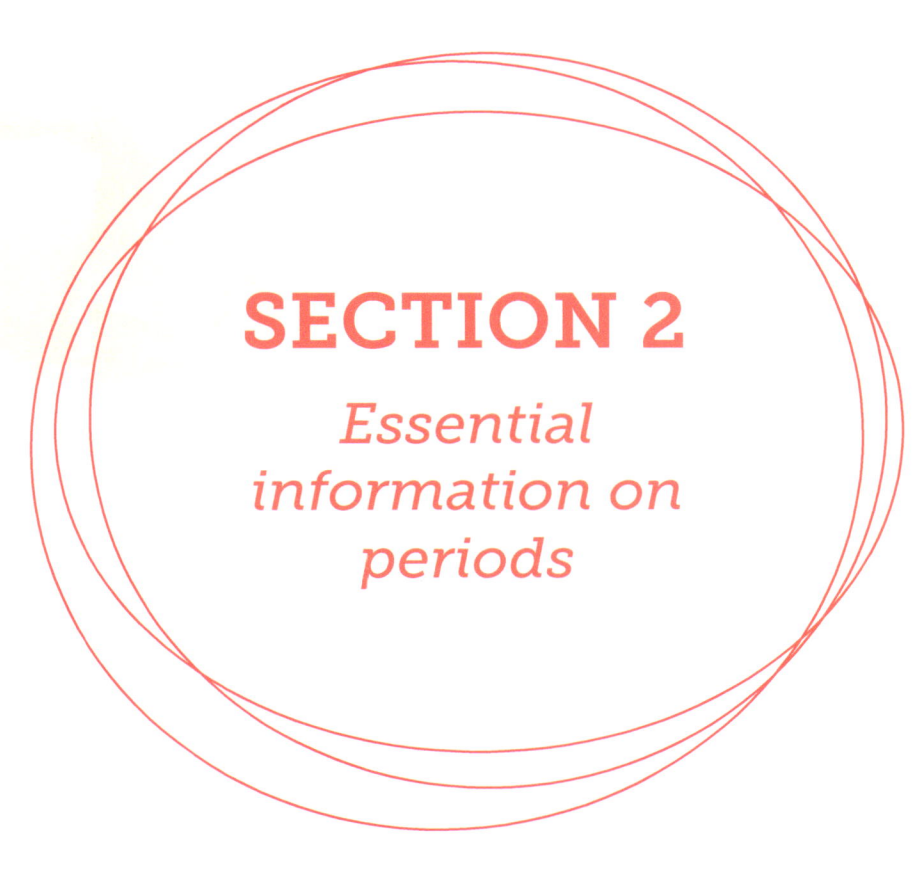

SECTION 2
Essential information on periods

QUICK QUESTIONS AND ANSWERS

What's a period?

Good question!

Here's the short answer—*a period* is the common name for something called ***menstruation***. This is the process of blood being released from a girl's uterus*, travelling down her vagina*, and out through her vulva*. This release of blood is called the menstrual flow. It happens for about five days, roughly every month for most girls and women.

* Uterus, vagina and vulva are organs within the female body You can see what they look like in the diagram on page 38.

Why do girls and women get periods?

The reason girls and women get periods is because the female anatomy is designed to create, house and birth babies, and the menstrual flow is a part of this process.

(For more detailed info see page 37.)

Do boys get periods?

No, boys and men don't get periods. It only happens to females.

When will I get my first period?

There's no way to know unfortunately. You are likely to have your first period sometime between 10 to 13 years old. This is the time that most girls get their first period. But you might get it earlier—at about 8 or 9 years old, or later—even up to 14 or 15 years old, or even later in some cases.

How often will I get a period?

Once you've had your first period, you can expect to get another period around once every month—usually about every 28 days. This is the typical time frame for most women to have a period. However for the first few years of getting your period, they might be less regular. So you may get your period after only 23 or 25 days, or maybe after 32, 35 or even 40 days. It might be different each month. This can be frustrating and annoying, as you are not sure when it will come. So it's a good idea to keep track of your period using a calendar or an app, to help you notice patterns in your own personal menstrual cycle.

(See page 54 for more information on tracking your period.)

How long does a period last?

A period usually lasts 5 days, but it may be shorter or longer, such as 3 or 8 days.

Why is it called a period?

It's not 100 percent certain why menstruation is called a period. It's most likely because it's the 'period of time' during your menstrual cycle where you release blood.

Do all women get a period?

Yes, the vast majority of women will get a period on a regular basis throughout their teenage and adult life.

(See page 69 for information about why someone might not get, or might stop getting, a period)

Got more quick questions?

I thought so. Make sure you read through the following sections for some more in-depth information. Then check out section 5 on page 63 for lots of other questions and answers.

WHY DO PERIODS HAPPEN?

To understand why girls and women get periods it's helpful to have an understanding of the female reproductive organs.

Inside of our body we all have organs, which play important roles in making our bodies function properly. You probably know some of them:

- **Your stomach**—which stores and processes the food you eat,
- **Your lungs**—which control your breathing,
- **Your heart**—which pumps blood around your veins and arteries.

Both boys and girls have these organs.

But there are some special organs that *only* girls have. They're called the *female reproductive organs*, and I've included a picture of them on the next page. (Since they're inside your body it's hard to know what they look like!)

One of the female reproductive organs is called the *uterus*. It sits inside your body below your belly button, in between your hip bones. It's a funny shape, kind of like an upside down triangle. Just like every other organ in your body, the uterus has a very important job that only it can do. It's where babies grow inside a woman's body.

Have you noticed that only women get pregnant and grow big bellies to have babies? Men can't do this because they don't have a uterus.

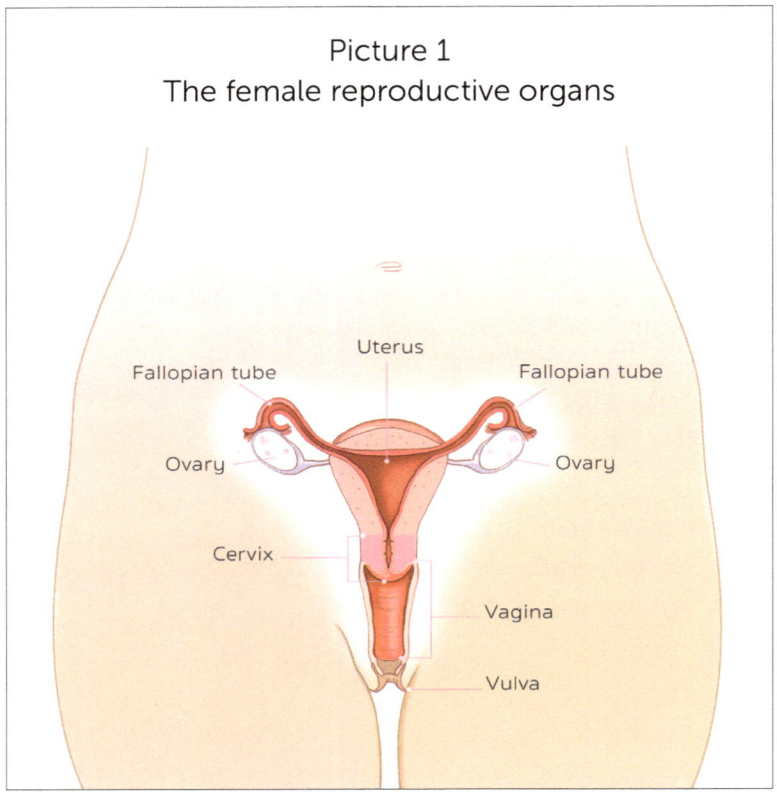

Picture 1
The female reproductive organs

As you can imagine, growing a baby is a very important job. The uterus needs to be working really well to get that job right, so it starts practising early.

Here's what it does:

You know how blood is important to keep us alive and healthy as people?

Well, babies need blood too, even when they're growing inside of a woman's body. This blood isn't the same blood that is pumped around the body by the heart, instead it's a special blood called 'menstrual blood' which lines the walls of the uterus and makes it a squooshy and safe place for the baby to live for 9 months.

Once a girl is old enough and starts puberty, the uterus gets busy practicing this process, so that it's ready to house a baby when she is older and is ready to have a baby. The girl's body grows lots of blood and stores it, lining all sides of the uterus to make that a safe, comfy home for a potential baby. Check out picture 2—you can see the dark red section—the thick lining of blood in the uterus.

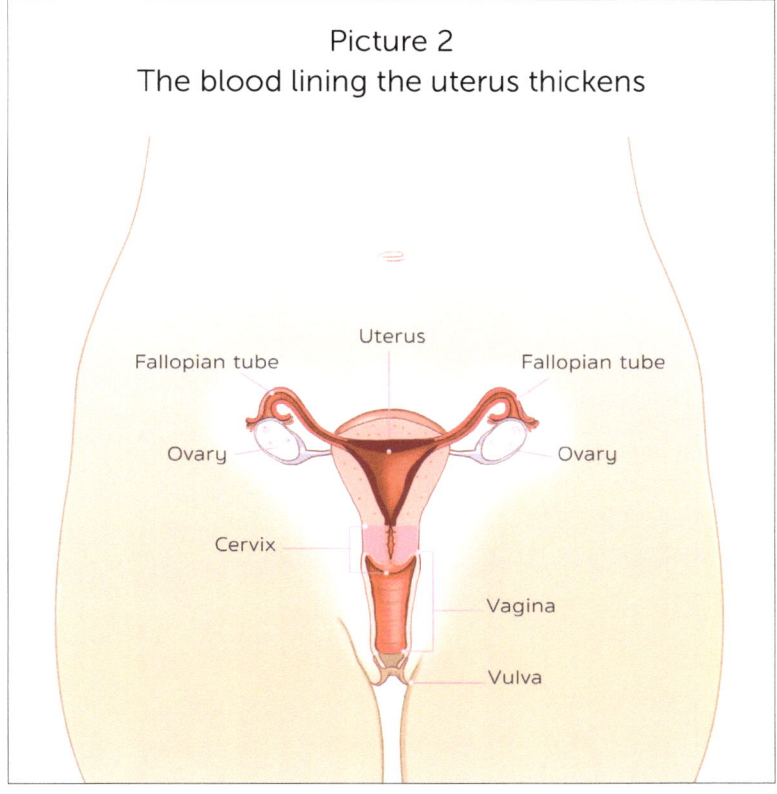

Picture 2
The blood lining the uterus thickens

After about a month of making and storing blood, and when the body realises there's no baby in the uterus—

it decides to get rid of all that blood, removing it from the uterus so it can start collecting fresh, new blood, ready for next month.

When the uterus decides to get rid of all that blood, it drains down a pipe called the vagina and flows out of our body, through the vulva (which is the opening to the vagina). And that's what a period is. It's when the unneeded 'menstrual blood' from your uterus is released from the body, through your vagina.

Picture 3 shows this.

Generally, a girl will lose about 30-40ml of blood each period. That's about 6-8 teaspoons in total over the 5 days.

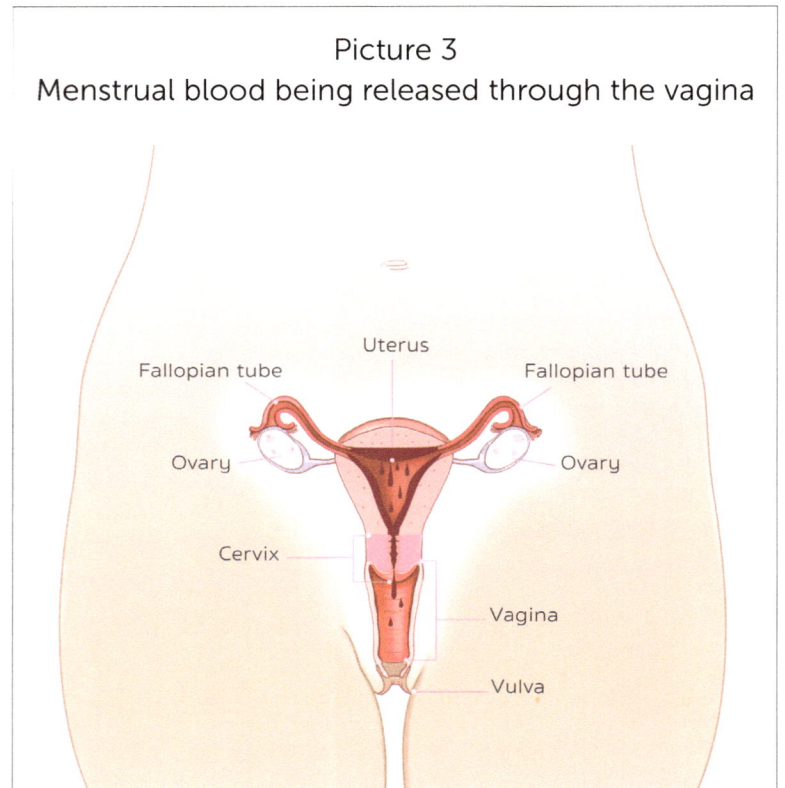

Picture 3
Menstrual blood being released through the vagina

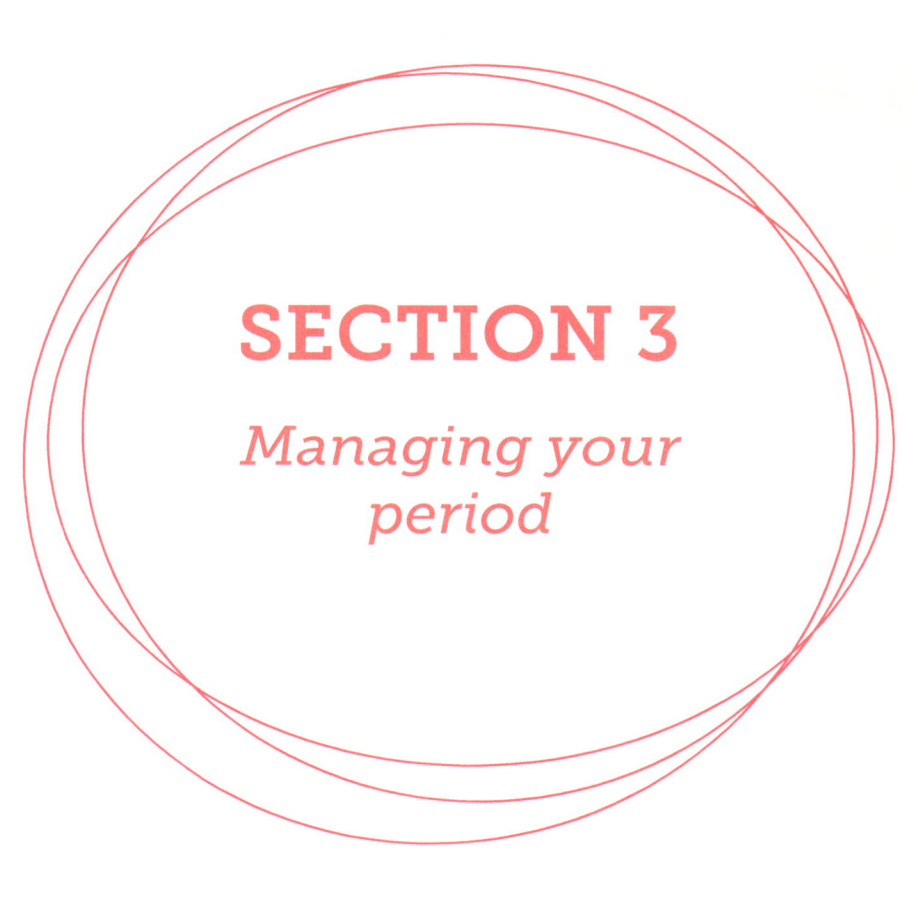

So a period means blood.

Blood can be messy, which means periods can be messy. Luckily, in our modern world we have many products that can help us to manage our periods. These are usually called 'feminine hygiene products', 'sanitary items' or 'sanitary products'.

But what do 'hygiene' and 'sanitary' mean?

Hygiene and sanitary are very similar meaning words. They both refer to:

> *"The process of keeping yourself and your surroundings clean, especially in order to keep yourself and others healthy, and prevent illness or the spread of diseases."*

So, when people refer to items such as pads or tampons as a 'sanitary item', a 'hygiene product' or a 'feminine hygiene product', they're using those terms because those items are specifically designed to keep girls and women clean and healthy during their period.

In this section of the book I'll be talking about the two main topics related to managing your period.

- THE FIRST is having ways to trap and collect the blood that flows out of your vulva, before it leaks out onto your underwear, down your legs and gets onto clothes and furniture. We call this *'using sanitary items'*.

- THE SECOND part is being aware of when your period is due to occur so you can be prepare. We call this *'tracking your menstrual cycle'*.

Using sanitary items

Here's an explanation of some of the sanitary products you might use to manage your period. Deciding which products to use is a personal choice, and it may take you a while to trial a few different products to find out what suits you.

PADS

These are absorbent pads of cotton that are worn inside your knickers. They absorb and hold blood after it flows down your vagina and out of your vulva.

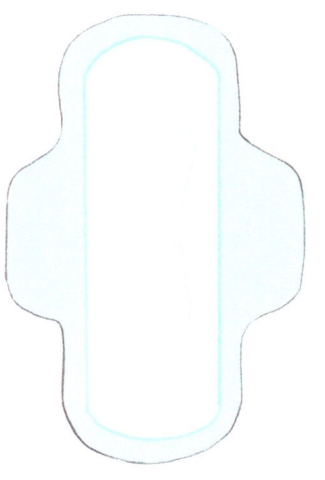

- Pads come in many different brands and sizes, but they are usually white, and long and oval in shape.

- Pads come in different levels of 'absorbency', which means they can hold different amounts of fluid, or menstrual blood. 'Light absorbency' can hold only a small amount of blood, while 'highly absorbent' or 'super absorbent' can hold a lot more blood.

Most modern pads will have a sticky side underneath them. This helps you attach the pad to your knickers, and hold it in place.

Some pads have extra bits at the side, called wings, which wrap around your knickers to hold it even more securely and prevent leaking. *To be hygienic and avoid unpleasant smells (odour), pads should be changed roughly every 3 to 4 hours, though you may wear them for longer overnight.*

When you might want to use a pad

Pads are the most commonly used sanitary items. Even women who regularly use tampons and menstrual cups are likely to also use a pad at other times.

When you first start getting your period you'll probably use pads more than other sanitary items as they can be simpler and less daunting to use than tampons or menstrual cups.

Pads are safe and effective to wear at most times during your period. It is best to choose an absorbency of pad to match your flow, eg. a 'super' pad on heavy days and a 'regular' pad on lighter days. It is also a good idea to wear an 'overnight' pad to bed at night. These are longer and more absorbent, so you are less likely to leak while sleeping for extended times, especially if you're a restless sleeper and move around a lot while you sleep.

When you might NOT want to wear a pad

- When you're swimming. Pads are very absorbent and when they get wet they increase in size. Wearing a wet pad would be very uncomfortable, bulky, and messy. You might want to choose a tampon, menstrual cup, or period swimwear instead.

- When you're wearing brief, or revealing clothing (such as a leotard for gymnastics, dancing or ice-skating, or a netball uniform). Again you might want to use a tampon for these activities, or choose an 'active' style of pad which is thinner and narrower than a typical pad. It can also help to 'double up' on underwear. eg. attach the pad to one pair of underwear, and wear a larger, firmer pair of briefs or a leotard over the top.

PANTY LINERS

Panty liners are similar to pads in their shape and construction, but they are much thinner and lighter and often smaller. This also means they are less absorbent, so they don't hold as much blood. *Panty liners should also be changed every 3 to 4 hours to ensure appropriate hygiene and to avoid unwanted odours.*

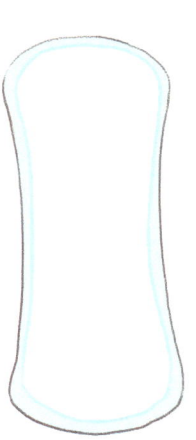

When you might want to use a liner

Because they're not very absorbent, liners are most commonly used as a 'back up'. This might be:

- instead of a pad or tampon,
- in the day or two before your period (in case it arrives early), or
- in the last day or two of your period (if you have just a small amount of spotting).

You might also want to wear a liner if you are wearing a tampon or menstrual cup and are worried about leaks due to a heavy flow. (See page 71 for an explanation of 'flow'.)

When you might NOT want to wear a liner

On the heavier days of your period. The liner won't absorb much menstrual blood and you are likely to leak blood onto your clothing.

TAMPONS

Tampons are small, firm cylindrical tubes made of tightly woven cotton. They are usually tapered (rounded) on one end, and flat, with a string attached to the other end.

Tampons are designed to be placed into your vagina with the rounded end first.

When inserting a tampon, you push it up through your vulva until it sits snugly inside your vagina. When you need to take the tampon out, you can pull the string down to remove the tampon easily.

Tampons should be changed every 3 to 4 hours to ensure appropriate hygiene and reduce the risk of infection. It is incredibly important that you don't wear tampons for extremely long periods of time as it can lead to a serious medical condition called 'toxic shock syndrome'.

On heavier flow days tampons may need to be changed more often. If you are leaking menstrual blood while wearing a tampon, it means that it might have reached its full absorbency and needs to be changed.

When you might want to use a tampon

Once you're familiar with inserting and removing a tampon, you might choose to use them at any time during your period. They are especially useful if you are going swimming, or going somewhere you might get wet, (eg. to a water park).

They are also very useful if you're doing physical activity where you are moving around quickly, or wearing something brief, eg. a leotard or running briefs. During these times a pad might feel bulky, or might move or fall out of your underwear, which could be embarrassing.

When you might NOT want to use a tampon.

You might not want to use a tampon in the initial months or years of getting your period if you're not feeling confident about inserting and removing it. You also shouldn't use a tampon overnight, or for longer than 3 to 4 hours at a time, as this can cause an increased risk of infection.

MENSTRUAL CUPS

Menstrual cups are a small device shaped like an egg cup, with a small straight stem at the base. They are most often made of medical grade silicon, or rubber.

Menstrual cups are designed to be inserted into the vagina, where they fit snugly, much like a tampon, and collect blood inside the bowl of the cup. They are then removed by grasping and pulling the stem down and out of your vagina. The blood will then need to be emptied out of the cup and cleaned/rinsed before reinserting.

Menstrual cups can be tricky to use initially, so if you want to start using one it's a good idea to practice at home first. They also need to be cleaned effectively, so you will need to make sure you have something to clean and store a used menstrual cup, to keep it hygienic.

When might you want to use a menstrual cup

A menstrual cup can be used at most times during your menstrual cycle, including:

- playing sport,
- when swimming, or
- overnight.

Many women choose to use menstrual cups because they are reusable, which means they are more ecofriendly than single use sanitary items such as pads, liners and tampons, which contribute waste to landfill.

Menstrual cups can be used for up to 12 hours without changing, so they can be quite convenient. However, you may need to change them every 3 to 4 hours on days where your flow is heavy, as the cup may get full more quickly.

When might you NOT want to use a menstrual cup?

If you don't feel comfortable managing the insertion or removal of a menstrual cup, if you have a physical disability that makes this difficult, or if you don't have access to appropriate facilities to hygienically clean and store your cup, (eg. when camping). You should also avoid using a menstrual cup if you have any kind of allergic reaction to the cup. Especially if it is a rubber latex style cup, rather than silicone.

It is also important to find a cup that fits correctly, or it won't effectively collect menstrual blood and may be uncomfortable, or irritating.

PERIOD UNDERWEAR

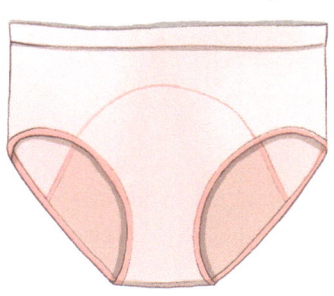

These are a special type of underwear that have an absorbent lining sewn into the gusset (the part between your legs) that collects and absorbs menstrual blood. This absorbent lining also includes a waterproof layer, so that the collected menstrual blood doesn't leak through the underwear.

Period underwear are designed to be worn and then washed in the washing machine before using again. There are many brands of period underwear on the market, in different styles, colours and absorbencies.

When might you want to use period underwear

Period underwear:

- can be worn anytime during your period, and during most activities.
- can be worn alone, or as a 'back up' if you are using tampons or a menstrual cup.

If you are wearing period underwear alone, you will need to change them at least every 12 hours (or more often if you have a heavy flow day or they begin to produce an odour).

It is important to choose the absorbency of period underwear that best matches your menstrual flow for that day. You can also purchase overnight styles of period underwear, which have larger and more absorbent gusset areas to prevent leaking while sleeping.

When might you NOT want to use period underwear

You might not want to wear these underwear while swimming (though there are period swimwear options available).

You might also choose not to wear period underwear at times when you have limited access to washing facilities, such as when travelling, or camping.

SANITARY DISPOSAL BAGS

These are small plastic bags with handles (similar to nappy or dog poo disposal bags). They are designed so that you can place a used disposable sanitary item—such as a tampon, pad or liner—in the bag and tie it up securely before disposing of it.

They are particularly useful if you don't have access to a sanitary disposal bin and need to store used items for a while until you can find a bin to dispose of them.

These bags are often scented to mask any odour of used sanitary items. You don't need to use these specific bags, you can easily use dog poo or nappy bags instead.

If you have access to a sanitary disposal bin, you can just pop the used item in there unwrapped, or wrapped in toilet paper. You can also use the wrapper of a pad or liner to wrap used items before disposal.

AN IMPORTANT NOTE ABOUT DISPOSING OF SANITARY ITEMS

Whichever type of sanitary item you choose to use, it is important to always dispose of them correctly:

- in a sanitary disposal bin, or
- hygienically wrapped and placed in a normal bin.

You should NEVER, ever flush a pad, tampon or panty liner down the toilet. They are too big to move through the plumbing and will clog the pipes. This can cause toilets to overflow and make a huge mess, which can be very costly to fix. Always dispose of sanitary items appropriately.

A FINAL NOTE ABOUT HYGIENE

Whatever form of sanitary product you choose to use, it's important to remember the number one rule of period hygiene. **Always make sure you wash your hands, before and after handling and changing your sanitary items.** This is important to keep your hands clean, protect your clothing and belongings from stains, and prevent the spread of infection.

Making a period kit

During puberty, it can be a really good idea to make yourself a period kit so you're prepared for when your period comes. You might even want to make two kits, one for at home, and one for in your school bag.

If you live at two places, such as if your parents are separated, or you spend time living at your grandparents, or in foster care, you might want to create a period kit for each home you live in.

A period kit is a small bag that contains the items you will need to manage your period. If you haven't yet got your period, it might be a good idea to have a kit like this in your school bag, just in case you get your period at school (like Piper did in the story).

If you've already had your first period it's a good idea to keep packing this kit and taking it in your bag on the few days before and during your period, so you will always have enough sanitary products to manage your period all day. You will need to restock your kit with products each night during your period, to replace the items you've used during the day.

What you will need:

A small bag, such as a toiletry bag, a pencil case, or a drawstring bag.

- a spare pair of underwear.
- 3-4 pads (if you use them)
- 3-4 tampons (if you use them)
- 3-4 liners (if you use them)
- 3-4 sanitary disposal bags (for disposing of used items)

Keeping track of when you will get your period

Remember how I said you are likely to have your period every 28 days? It's helpful to know this information, because it means you can predict when your next period might start.

This is called:

- 'tracking your period',
- 'tracking your menstrual cycle', or
- 'tracking your cycle'.

Why would you want to track your menstrual cycle?

The most important reason for tracking your cycle is so you know when your next period is likely to start.

This means you can be prepared with pads and other sanitary items around this time. For example, you might choose to wear a panty liner, or a pair of period underwear the day or two before your period is due (to catch any blood in case it comes early).

It's also a good time to check your stocks of period products (such as pads, tampons, etc.) to make sure you have enough to get you through to your next period. You don't want to find that you've got your period in the middle of the night and then discover that you've run out of pads or tampons. That would be stressful and uncomfortable. It's best to be prepared.

How can I track my period?

There are two main ways you can track your period:

1. Use a period chart—such as the one below. It's a calendar where you make a note of the days you have your period. You then count up 28 days from the first day of your last period to make a note of the day your next period is likely to be due.

Sample period chart/tracker

SUNDAY	MONDAY	TUESDAY	WEDNESDAY	THURSDAY	FRIDAY	SATURDAY
		FIRST DAY OF PERIOD (DAY 1)	DAY 2	DAY 3	DAY 4	DAY 5
1	2	3	4	5	6	7
DAY 6	DAY 7	DAY 8	DAY 9	DAY 10	DAY 11	DAY 12
8	9	10	11	12	13	14
DAY 13	DAY 14	DAY 15	DAY 16	DAY 17	DAY 18	DAY 19
15	16	17	18	19	20	21
DAY 20	DAY 21	DAY 22	DAY 23	DAY 24	DAY 25	DAY 26
22	23	24	25	26	27	28
DAY 27	DAY 28	NEXT PERIOD DUE				
29	30	31	1	2	3	4

2. Use a period tracking app, these work by you inputting data into the app about when you get your period, and then the app automatically predicts when your next period might be due. Some current popular apps include the following:

    - Clue, Period Diary, Flo and Eve
    - Many smart-watches, such as a Garmin or Fitbit, might also have a period tracker function

SECTION 4

Other ways to take care of yourself while you have your period

What is self-care?

Keeping clean and healthy (remember that word 'hygiene') is really important when you have your period. But something else that's also important is being more aware of 'self-care' during this time.

Some people call 'self-care' by lots of other names. They might say, 'taking care of myself', 'looking after myself', having some 'me time'.

Getting your first period is a big change for many girls. Some girls find this change an easy adjustment. Others find this new part of their lives a bit overwhelming, intimidating or worrying. Your response is going to be as individual as you are.

It's important to remember that your period is a big task for your body, so you may feel a bit more worn out or tired around the time you have your period.

You may also experience what is called 'pre-menstrual syndrome' or PMS for short. This is a collection of physical and emotional symptoms you might have in the few days before your period arrives, and the first few days of your period. Sometimes PMS is known as PMT, short for pre-menstrual tension. PMS and PMT generally mean the same thing.

Symptoms of Pre-Menstrual Syndrome

Emotions and feelings:

The following feelings and emotions are all typical during PMS, particularly if they seem to show up for no apparent reason.

- Grumpy
- Tired
- Angry or irritable
- Annoyed
- Sad or weepy
- Frustrated

Physical and other body symptoms:

The following physical symptoms are all a typical part of PMS.

- Aches or cramps in your stomach and abdomen
- Bloating or fluid retention
- Food cravings or change in appetite
- Headaches
- Hot flushes or sweats
- Increased sensitivity to sounds, light and touch
- Tender or aching breasts

All of these symptoms are very common and normal experiences around the time of your period. Most of them can be addressed with some simple self-care.

Self-care ideas

Now that you know it's a good idea to take a bit more special care of yourself when you have your period, you need some 'self-care' ideas. Here are a few you can try:

- Have a rest with a hot water bottle or warm wheat pack on your belly
- Go for a walk around the block

- Do some yoga, pilates or gentle stretching

- Get more sleep—go to bed a bit earlier if you can, or take an afternoon nap if it fits into your schedule

- Put on a diffuser with your favourite essential oils

- Put on your favourite music and have a mini-dance party in your bedroom

- Snuggle up on the couch or bed and read a book

- Have a movie night and watch something funny

- Call your best friend for a chat

- Take a bubble bath or put on a face mask

- Do some meditation or mindfulness—try the Smiling Mind or Headspace apps

Remember that PMS is normal part of having your period. However, sometimes these symptoms can become a bit more of a problem for some girls and women. If you're finding these symptoms are causing you lots of pain or distress, or are stopping you from doing the things you love or want to do, then remember to talk to a trusted adult about your concerns.

SECTION 5

A bunch of other questions about periods you might want answered

What's puberty?

In this book I've talked about menstruation, which I've said is a normal part of puberty. But what's puberty? Well, puberty is simply the time in a person's life when their body changes from that of a child, to that of an adult.

Puberty happens to all girls and boys. It generally starts around ages 8 to 10, and lasts for several years into the mid teenage years. Puberty consists of many body changes.

For girls this means the start of menstruation, but also the development of breasts, widening of hips, as well as growth of pubic hair near your genitals and in your armpits.

Puberty might also mean changes in mood, body odour and other changes such as being interested in having a romantic relationship, or wanting more independence in your life.

Does a period mean I'm hurt or injured?

No, menstruation is a completely normal part of being a female. Each month, when you get your period, it means that your body is working exactly as it should be.

Menstrual blood is different to other blood that lives inside our bodies. The 'rest of our body' blood is supposed to stay inside our body. When it doesn't, that can sometimes be a concern.

Have you ever seen blood? Maybe you fell over and scraped your knee; or cut your fingers on a pair of scissors or maybe you got bumped in the nose and got a nosebleed. Most of the time when 'rest of our body' blood comes outside of our body it's a sign that we're hurt, or unwell, so it can be a little scary or painful.

But 'menstrual blood' is different. When menstrual blood comes out of our body, it's not because we're hurt or sick. It's actually a sign that our body - especially our uterus - is working exactly as it should be!

Will a period be painful?

Usually, no. The process of blood leaving your uterus and draining out your vagina should not hurt. However, you might find that you get some mild pain and discomfort in your stomach and around your hips, around the time of, or just before, your period. This pain is generally muscle pain from the muscles of the uterus contracting to release the blood.

If you get a lot of pain during your period, or your pain is so bad it prevents you from doing things you have to do in your day, you should ask an adult to take you to speak to a pharmacist, nurse or GP (doctor).

My Mum got her period when she was 11 years old. Does this mean I'll get mine when I'm 11 too?

Not necessarily. Every girl's body is different, so the age your mother, or sister, or grandmother got their periods will not have a significant impact on the age that you will be when you get yours.

What are the signs that I might get my period soon?

You're likely to get it around two years after you first start to grow breasts.

Another clue you might be close to getting your period is you might start to notice a white sticky substance on your underwear. This is called a vaginal discharge and it's perfectly normal. It might be clear or a milky white colour. You might start to get this about six months before you get your first period.

Where can I buy or find sanitary products?

Most sanitary items, such as pads, tampons, panty liners, wipes and disposal bags are available at a wide range of stores, such as supermarkets, chemists and even petrol stations.

Most supermarkets have a whole section full of shelves especially for sanitary items. They are normally near other hygiene items, such as shampoo, soap and deodorant.

You can sometimes also find sanitary items in vending machines in public toilets.

Other sanitary items, such as period underwear or menstrual cups may be more difficult to find in stores, and may need to be purchased online.

If you find yourself needing emergency supplies of sanitary items (for example if your period arrives and you've forgotten to pack your period pack) your school is likely to have sanitary items available from the front office or sickbay.

Who can I go to for help if my period arrives unexpectedly?

You can't ever know when your first period will arrive. And even once you start getting our period, it might arrive early or late, which means you might be unprepared for it.

This is why it's important to know who you can go to for help if your period arrives unexpectedly. Here's a handy list of people you can go to for assistance, or to find some sanitary products:

- Your parents, or older sister (if she already has her period)

- Teachers and front office staff
- Your sports coach or team manager, Scouts or youth group leader
- If you're at the shops, a chemist assistant, or information desk assistant
- Your friends who you know already have their period, or older girls you know and trust
- Your aunty, grandmother, or older cousin
- If you're at a major event such as the show or fair, or big sporting matches, look for first aid officers
- If you're at the beach or pool, look for the lifeguards
- Don't forget, this list does not just include women. You can also ask men you know and trust, such as teachers or sports coaches, for help. (Though you might feel more comfortable asking another female.)

How long will I have my period?

As we mentioned before, you will probably start to get your period when you're between 10 and 13 years old. You will keep having a period until you reach about 45 to 55 years old. So you will probably have a period about once every month, for about 35 to 45 years. Yes! That's a long time.

What are the reasons my period might stop?

If you ever get pregnant, you will stop having a period for the time you are pregnant, and the several weeks afterwards. If you decided to breastfeed your baby, then you will probably not have a period for the first several months of breastfeeding.

Sometimes if you stop having your period, it means you might be stressed or unwell. If it doesn't come back after another month it is best to see your doctor.

When will I get my last period?

As mentioned previously, you will probably have your last period sometime around 45 to 55 years old. This time in your life, when you stop having periods, is called menopause. During menopause women's periods may be very inconsistent, for example they may only have a period once every 2 or 3 months. And eventually they will stop altogether. Once a woman's periods stop, she is no longer able to become pregnant and have a baby.

What if I don't want to get my period?

Unfortunately you don't get to choose to not have a period. It's a normal bodily function that serves an important role in our body. Just like peeing and pooping might be unpleasant, they still serve an important role. It's okay to feel like you don't want to have your period. Lots of girls and women feel this way. But it's also important to find ways to accept this new change.

Is there any way to stop me from having a period?

In certain circumstances, a doctor may be able to prescribe a medication which can stop girls and women from having periods. However, this is not a very common action and doctors will require important reasons to make this decision. It is something that is likely to be decided between a girl, her parents or guardians, and her doctor for medical reasons.

Will periods be different for me because of my autism?

No. The physical process of having your period won't be any different because of your autism. However, it's important to remember that periods can be different for lots of different girls. What might be different for you is that you might respond to getting your period differently.

If you have sensory sensitivities you may also have a few more difficulties finding menstrual products that feel comfortable for you. If so, you can ask an occupational therapist for help.

I'm feeling really scared about getting my first period? What should I do?

First of all, don't panic. It's perfectly normal to feel a little bit worried about lots of things during puberty, particularly about getting your period. If you're feeling worried, the best thing you can do is to talk to someone you trust about your worries, such as a parent or another trusted relative (maybe an aunty or grandmother, or an older sister or female cousin if you have one). You might also be able to talk to a trusted older friend, or a peer worker or support worker if you have one.

Am I allowed to talk about my period with other people?

Yes, it is okay to talk about your period with people you know and trust. Be aware that some people might find talking about periods uncomfortable because it is a bodily function. Some people might also not know much about periods, particularly people who are younger than you, or people who are boys.

What does 'flow' mean?

When people talk about periods, they might use the word flow to describe the bleeding (like I did earlier in the book). They might say 'light flow' or 'heavy flow'. What they mean by 'flow' is how much blood is flowing out of the vagina.

For example, a 'heavy flow' might mean that a lot of blood is coming out of the vagina, which means that your period might be filling up pads and tampons quite quickly.

A 'light flow' means that much less blood is coming out of your vagina, and you will see less blood collecting on pads and tampons, so you won't need to change them quite as often (though you will still need to change them about every 3 to 4 hours in order to keep hygienic).

A 'medium flow' is when the rate of bleeding is somewhere in between light and heavy.

You might also hear the term 'spotting' which is also related to flow. This means that there are just very small amounts of blood coming out of the vagina. This may look like spots of red or brown blood on pads or liners, hence the term 'spotting'.

THANK YOU, ACKNOWLEDGEMENTS & MORE INFORMATION

Thank you

Thank you to everyone who purchased and read this book. I truly hope I've answered a few of your questions, and that you're now feeling more confident and positive about navigating periods and puberty in the coming years.

For more information on the Well Girls program and Bloom Wellbeing Occupational Therapy, you can find us in the following places:

- **Bloom Wellbeing website:** bloomwellbeing.com.au
- **Instagram:** instagram.com/bloomwellbeing
- **Facebook:** facebook.com/bloomwellbeing

Acknowledgements

Writing a book rarely happens in isolation, which means I have many people to thank for their support in getting this book to print.

To all the 'Well Girls' (the participants in my Bloom Wellbeing 'Well Girls Program' over the past three years), thank you for being my motivation to write this book, and for continually inspiring me with your uniqueness, creativity, resilience and energy.

To every person who supported this book by pledging funding for it through the Kickstarter project. I feel so honoured by your faith in me and this book, and I thank you for your support.

To my Well Girls co-facilitator and partner in crime, Valeska Waldron, thank you for being part of the program and for bringing fresh ideas and perspectives to it.

To the rest of my Bloom Wellbeing team—Michelle, Sam, Maddi, Elliahn and Sarah—I couldn't have built this business without your support and hard work.

To my professional A-team—Joanna Connolly, Clare Crew, Carly Thompson-Barry—for being the best sounding-boards a girl could ask for.

To Rita Sus, thankyou for your incredible illustrations, and for bringing Piper to life in full colour.

To Kelly Exeter, for not only her exceptional book designing skills, but also her incredible patience with this deadline-wary writer.

And of course, to my family, Tyson, Ella and Maisie, for always understanding when I chose the laptop over family time. I promise to make it up to you now the book is done!

About the author

Sarah Hausler is an Occupational Therapist and director of Bloom Wellbeing, an Adelaide based Occupational Therapy clinic. Sarah is also a qualified journalist, and has previously written for and edited a range of publications, including parenting magazines. This is Sarah's first published book.

Information for parents and caregivers

Thank you for purchasing this book for a young woman in your life.

For the past three years I've been running the Well Girls puberty preparation and life skills program for girls with autism, through my business, Bloom Wellbeing.

While running this program I began to realise the need for a new kind of resource to help explain periods to girls with autism. Many of the mainstream books available on this topic can be difficult for girls with autism to access. They often include a lot of inferences, sarcasm and other elements which can make them tricky for girls with autism to decode. There's also a range of puberty texts available for girls with intellectual disabilities, but these can often be a little too simplistic in how much information they contain. If there's one thing I've learned in two years of running this program, it's that my participants have A LOT OF QUESTIONS!! So I wanted to create a text that was accessible, informative and useful.

Piper Gets Her Period has been written specifically to be easily accessed and understood by girls with autism, yet it's not ONLY for girls with autism. This book can just as easily be used for girls with other developmental, intellectual or cognitive difficulties, Downs Syndrome and other conditions, as well as neurotypical children of course.

www.ingramcontent.com/pod-product-compliance
Lightning Source LLC
Chambersburg PA
CBHW041500010526
44107CB00044B/1515